Symbols of Freedom

The Liberty Bell

Tristan Boyer Binns

Heinemann Library
Chicago, Illinois

© 2001 Reed Educational & Professional Publishing
Published by Heinemann Library,
an imprint of Reed Educational & Professional Publishing,
Chicago, IL

Customer Service 888-454-2279

Visit our website at www.heinemannlibrary.com

Designed by Lisa Buckley
Printed in Hong Kong

05 04 03
10 9 8 7 6

Library of Congress Cataloging-in-Publication Data
Binns, Tristan Boyer, 1968-
      The Liberty Bell / Tristan Boyer Binns.
         p. cm. -- (Symbols of freedom)
      Includes bibliographical references (p.) and index.
      ISBN 1-58810-119-3 (lib. bdg.)   ISBN 1-58810-403-6 (pbk. bdg.)
      1. Liberty Bell--Juvenile literature. I. Title.

   F158.8.I3 B56 2001
   974.8'11--dc21   00-058147

Acknowledgments
The author and publishers are grateful to the following for permission to reproduce copyright material: p.5 National Archives, p.6, 7, 10, 19, 25 Leif Skoogfors/Corbis, p.8 The Purcell Team/Corbis, p.9 13, 14, 21, 22 Bettmann/Corbis, p.11 Ted Spiegel/Corbis, p.12 Nanine Hartzenbusch/AP Photo, p.15, 26 Corbis, p.16 Galgonek/ Sovofoto/Eastfoto/PictureQuest, p.17 Adam Woolfitt/Corbis, p.18 Jean Leon Gerome Ferris/Wood River Gallery/ PictureQuest, p.20 Francis G. Mayer/Corbis, p.23 Bingham/Wood River Gallery/PictureQuest, p.24, 27, 28 Independence Hall National Historic Park, p.29 Kelly-Mooney Photography/Corbis.
Cover photograph by Leif Skoogfors/Corbis.

Some words are shown in bold, **like this.**
You can find out what they mean by looking in the glossary.

Contents

What Is the Liberty Bell?

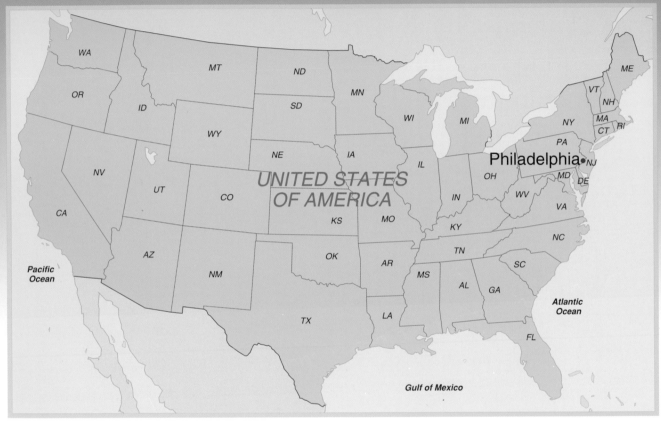

The **Liberty** Bell is a very large bell. It is kept in Philadelphia, Pennsylvania. It doesn't ring like a regular bell because it is cracked.

The Liberty Bell is a **symbol** of the freedom all
Americans enjoy. It helps people remember
the day that the **Declaration of Independence**
was first read aloud.

Looking at the Liberty Bell

The **Liberty** Bell is made of **copper,** tin, silver, gold, and other metals. It hangs on a wooden **yoke.**

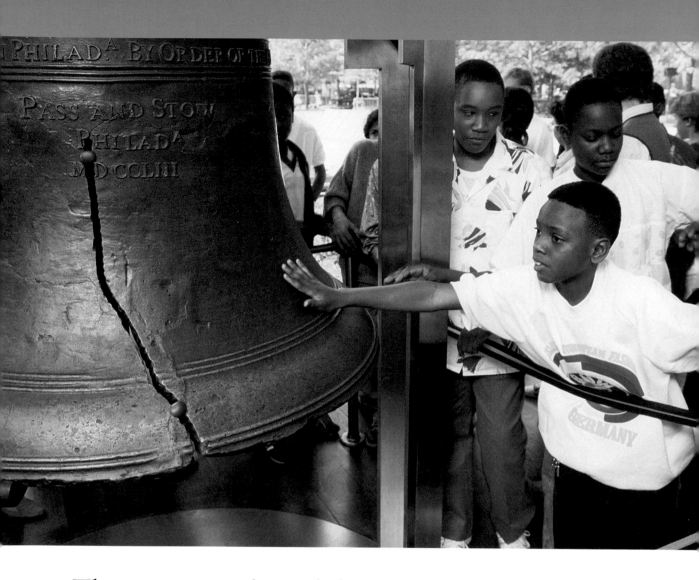

There are words and dates on the bell.
The words are from the **Bible.** They tell
about freedom for all people.

A Famous Shape

The **Liberty** Bell's shape is famous. There have been cookie jars, teapots, and even a hot-air balloon in the shape of the Liberty Bell!

The Liberty Bell has been on stamps and money. One of the first **space capsules** was called the *Liberty Bell 7*.

Millions of people visit the **Liberty** Bell each year. It is part of the **Independence** National **Historic** Park. It can be seen any time of day or night.

The Liberty Bell is in a park across the street from Independence Hall. It was moved to its new home in 1976, our country's 200th birthday.

Ringing the Bell

The **Liberty** Bell is **struck** at very important times. In 1996, it was struck to celebrate Dr. Martin Luther King's birthday.

The Liberty Bell has sounded at other times, too. At the end of **World War II,** the bell was struck. People around the United States listened to the sound on the radio.

A Bell for Philadelphia

Three hundred years ago there were no
telephones, radios, or televisions. People
gathered when they heard a bell ring. Then
someone would read important news out loud.

Every town had a bell. But Philadelphia was the **capital** of Pennsylvania. It was a very important city. So the **colonists** of Pennsylvania wanted a very large bell for their State House.

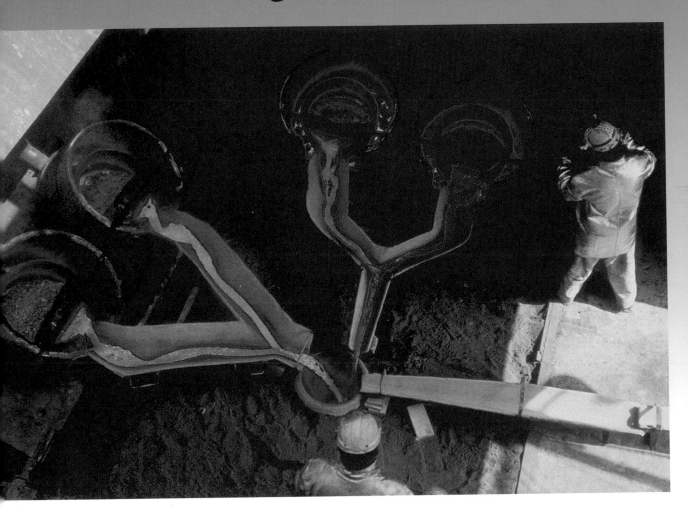

No one in the **colonies** could make a big bell. The **colonists** had to order it from England. This modern picture shows how the bell was **cast** in a hole dug in the ground.

16

First, a **mold** for the bell was made. The words on the bell were part of the mold. Liquid metal was poured into the mold. Bells are still made this way today.

In 1752, the bell was sent to Philadelphia. It was taken to **Independence** Hall. The people wanted to hear the bell ring. But when it rang, it cracked!

Two men named Pass and Stow melted down the bell and made a new one. But people did not like its sound. The men had to start over. The third bell is the one we have today.

On July 4, 1776, the **Congress** met in Philadelphia. They adopted the **Declaration of Independence.** It said that the **colonies** would become one **independent** country.

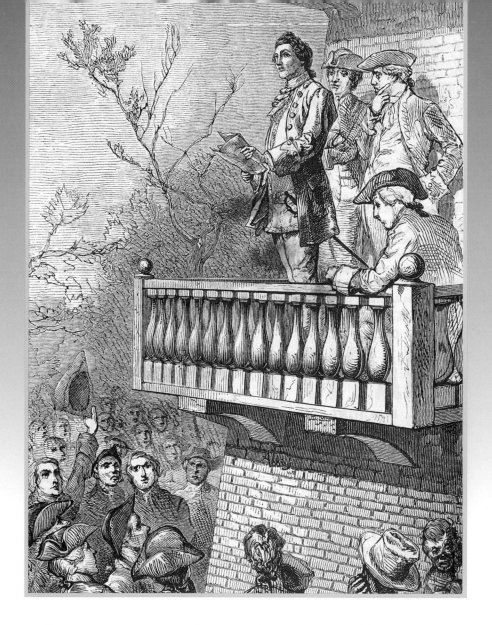

On July 8, 1776, the **Liberty** Bell rang to call the **colonists** to Independence Hall. A man read the Declaration of Independence out loud.

The **colonists** fought the **Revolutionary War** against Britain to become **independent.** During the war, the British captured the city of Philadelphia.

The colonists moved all the bells out of the city. A farmer took the **Liberty** Bell to Allentown, Pennsylvania. It was hidden in a church. After the war, it was taken back to Philadelphia.

The Famous Crack

In 1835, the **Liberty** Bell cracked while it was ringing. Workers tried to fix the crack by filing down the edges.

In 1846, the Liberty Bell rang to celebrate George Washington's birthday. A big zigzag crack raced up the bell. It was ruined and could never ring again. Instead, it was put on display in **Independence** Hall.

The **Liberty** Bell has traveled thousands of miles! During the 1800s, it traveled by train to New Orleans, Chicago, and Atlanta. Later, it traveled to Boston and St. Louis.

In 1915, the Liberty Bell went on its last tour. It was taken to San Francisco for a huge fair. Crowds of people came to see it. Then it was taken home to **Independence** Hall.

In the Past

Before 1839, the **Liberty** Bell was called the "State House Bell." Then a picture of the bell was used on a booklet about freedom for slaves. The booklet called it the "Liberty Bell."

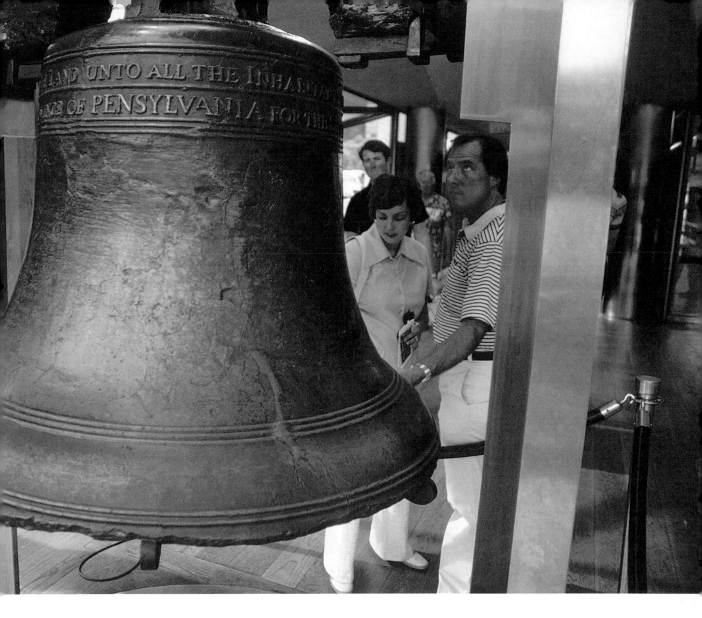

The men who made the first bell spelled
Pennsylvania wrong. Even though the bell
was **cast** again, no one changed the spelling.
Today it still says "Pensylvania."

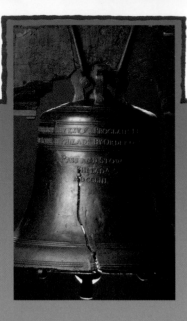

Liberty Bell

★ The **Liberty** Bell weighs as much as a pickup truck.

★ The crack in the Liberty Bell is almost as long as a yardstick!

★ The bell's **clapper** is as long as a baseball bat. It weighs as much as a small child.

★ The **yoke** for the Liberty Bell is made of a wood called Slippery Elm.

Glossary

Bible book of Christian holy writings

capital important city where the government is located

cast to pour a liquid into a shape and let it harden

clapper moving part inside a bell that hits the sides

colonist someone who is part of a group of people who move to a faraway land

colony group of people who move to a faraway land but who are still under the rule of the country they came from

Congress group of people who are elected to make the laws for the United States

copper soft, reddish-brown metal that is easy to shape

Declaration of Independence paper that says that America is a separate country from Britain

historic place that is famous because something important happened there in the past

independence being apart from anyone else's rule

independent not ruled or controlled by another country

liberty freedom to choose your work, your religion, and your friends

mold empty container that is made into a shape and then has hot liquid poured inside it to form something else

Revolutionary War war that the thirteen colonies fought against Britain in the 1700s to become a separate country

space capsule small vehicle early astronauts used to explore outer space

struck was hit

symbol something that stands for an idea

World War II war that was fought in Europe and in Asia during the 1940s

yoke wooden frame

More Books to Read

An older reader can help you with these books:

Sakurai, Gail. *The Liberty Bell*. Danbury, Conn.: Children's Press, 1996.

Wilson, Jon. *The Liberty Bell: Sounds of Freedom*. Chanhassen, Minn.: The Child's World, 1998.

Index